The Man Who
Could Freeze Time

The Man Who
Could Freeze Time

POEMS BY

Charles Darling

iUNIVERSE, INC.

New York
Lincoln
Shanghai

The Man Who Could Freeze Time

iUniverse books may be ordered through booksellers or by contacting:

iUniverse
2021 Pine Lake Road, Suite 100
Lincoln, NE 68512
www.iuniverse.com
1-800-Authors (1-800-288-4677)

Because of the dynamic nature of the Internet, any Web addresses or links contained in this book may have changed since publication and may no longer be valid.

ISBN: 978-0-595-44827-2 (pbk)
ISBN: 978-0-595-89144-3 (ebk)

Printed in the United States of America

Text and cover designer: Barbara Bachman
Production consultant: Richard Elman
Editorial consultants: Bill Sabin and Pat Haskell

For Marylynn,

with love—forever.

Even longer than that.

Contents

The Man Who
Could Freeze Time

Bahner's Funeral Home

— Summer 1954

In Loup City, Nebraska, we lived next door to
Bahner's Funeral Home,
a sprawl of white stucco and red tiles
set over a great brown lawn containing
a circle of roses—no trees—
and two of those silver balls on concrete posts
and a sundial that never seemed to work
by a child's reckoning.

Inside a garage out back
there lurked a wooden-sided station wagon
which triple-served as ambulance,
hearse, and sometimes family car.
Nothing, I must tell you, ever stirred the blood
of an eight-year-old like Mr. Bahner's
Plymouth wagon charging down the driveway,
hot on death-or-near-death's tail,
the limestone gravel scattering like shark's teeth,
the siren squalling like a child bereft.

Afterwards, Mrs. Bahner
showed us boys how to stretch
the sheets across the sun-drenched grass
to bleach away the stains,
rigging the yard with fallen sails.

We'd make up stories then of things
we knew nothing about: highway horrors,
barroom murders, river drownings.

One time Mikey Bahner showed me
the casket room. The satin pillows,
the cold brass handles and finials,
the caskets' awful heft upon our hands—
it all felt good to us, rich and clean,
and smelled like something metallic, unexplained,
found in an old church cellar, something
too important for boys to touch.
So, no matter what he said,
I would not close the casket's upper half
against Mikey's face when he
lay down in one.

Once, that last summer
before our family moved away,
Mike and I stole into the curtained front room
to see a boy, our age, we didn't know
who'd been surprised to death by his
brother's aimless gesture with a gun.
I remember nothing half so well
as the steadfast blueness of his suit,
the purse of his small mouth,
a pale pink spot above his eye.

Then, when we spilled ourselves outside again
to a smell of roses gone heavy in the yard,
to the motes slow-dancing in
Nebraska's shimmering afternoon,
to a spangling of sunshine,
then we were running, running, running,
until we knew that we could run no more.

Home-Made

A drop of oil on rusty gears,
the ritual of grey salt
and handfuls of ice chips
layered up to tub-top.
And the cranking, easy at first,
even for sisters, then hard
until my arm burns and the palm
that holds the freezer still
is embedded backward
with the Eskimo word for Eskimo.

We add salt and ice, crank
until a father's wrist
can give it only one more turn
and saltwater flows
down the back porch steps.
After hamburgers and corn-on-the-cob,
we pull out the dasher
dripping with flecks
of vanilla, add the ministry
of peaches or berries.
Then the first spoonfuls and
remembering too late
that exquisite pain behind the eyes.

Provisions

My mother put the summer up in jars,
tomatoes, beans, and corn,
succotash, piccalilli.
Hostages held against winter need—
essence of ache and dirt,
knead and coax of hoe and plow,
runnels of dew of cabbage leaf—
all consigned to clink of glass, lid jingle,
caught in the morning hymn of steam.

Come February, in the cellar,
I'd steal beyond the hydra-like furnace
where it lorded it over the dark
and enter the little room my father built
of new pine boards for mother's jars.
In incandescent dustiness
I'd choose a jar of peach preserves,
tip the wax seal, jam my fingers in;
then, laved in the smell of summer lost,
I'd catch it whole again upon my tongue.

Painting by Number

—Christmas 1954

I dipped my brush carefully
in the little capsules, numbered and named—
mocha, tan, sepia, cervine—
painting a horse's head in shades of brown.
I stayed within the lines,
made sure every space
that called for number four, a chestnut brown,
got number four before I moved to number five—
up to that spot of carmine red
in the corner of its dark, liquescent eye.

My sister painted a village square,
gabled and steepled and perfectly bright—
pink splashes in flowerboxes, golden acacias,
town hall flags in cerulean air.
Or so it appeared on the box. But my sister
painted things the way she wanted them—
mixing colors, ignoring lines,
putting in what wasn't there but what
she thought the little town should have:
fountains of green in a yellow square,
laundry hung by the churchyard door,
lavender birds in a lemonwood sky.

I said there never was a place
that looked like that, but our uncle
said he saw it in the war:
"Ça c'est la Ville D'Argentat.
C'est dans le sud de la France."

I was ten, my sister eight, that year.
I wish I could remember whether
it was what my uncle said
or the plain fact of an honest horse
lost in a variegated dream of France
that taught me truth in art is earned
by learning how to fabricate.

Tornado: A Memory of Wynnewood

Each spring, the warm Gulf air
arranged to meet a front
sweeping down the plains from Canada
and in the twisted wedding sheets
spawned storms—the very thing we waited for.

Tornadoes spared the town I lived in as a boy;
they chose the next town over, Wynnewood.
We knew the signs: the yellow sky,
the burned-fuse smell of stagnant air,
the roar like far-off trains.
And the stories afterward:
how one farmer's horse endured
a quick but ghostly transmigration
to a neighbor's field,
how another found a piece
of barn door wood through which
a stalk of timothy was driven like a nail.

One year, my family drove to Wynnewood
to see the ruin twisters made when
they hit the lumber yard. And not a house
left standing didn't have a sheet of plywood
sticking from its roof like a shark's tooth
or two-by-fours projecting through its walls
like whiskers. But one place queenly sat,
the shell completely gone, its furniture,

like the stuff you see in high school plays,
arranged exactly as it was before
the roof and wall went somewhere else—
as if the tables, chairs, and lamps were trying
to recall how it felt to belong to a home,
expecting it back any time.

In the Alleghenies, One Night

—For F.H.P. Jr.

It had something to do with being boys,
that night in the Alleghenies,
where the stream declined to a gravelly field,
to valley sleepiness, white water gone,
and we laid a fire by Tionesta's lazy song.
On the other side, in hemlock silhouettes
darkness brewed, and though we were boys,
we talked of dying, how we thought it would be.
I said it's like the heat that waits in wood
and will get out, come soon or late;
Howard wished it quick, as a leaping trout
will snatch a glint of silver from the air;
David, though, would grow old and fine,
as a buck one year will stay in a high place,
settling his bones to the ground like snow.

As flames died down, the stars grew bright.
Howard was first to see one fall, then another,
but no one wished for anything out loud.
Before we left, we threw the coals
in vermilion arcs to the river; a hiss,
then steam, rising and falling like ghosts,
moving downstream. We picked our way
through ferns and boulders to the road.

Somewhere a dog barked, and behind us
the river's song became a whispering—
like a shy father telling a secret,
something he nearly forgot to say,
something to do with being a boy.

In the Back of Comic Books

In the back of comic books were ads
for sea monkeys, whoopee cushions, magic tricks,
growing rocks, whole bags of exotic stamps,
ways to make money guaranteed by selling grit,
and the Charles Atlas Bull Worker.
I ordered it in March. By June,
I figured, let them try to bother us,
me and the girlfriend I had yet to meet on the beach.

Then watch me rise, arms and shoulders
spreading out like wings in the sun,
muscle popping out of muscle,
biceps, triceps, pecs, and abs.
By July, August, at the latest,
I'd show those bastards how to loom.

Night Riding in the Season of Goat's Thorn

All we wanted that summer night
was one smooth ride down valley shadow—
the wind to flatten back our hair,
tires to sing on a still-hot road.

Goat's thorn nailed the new front tire
and put an end to the first descent
down Choctaw Hill—the bicycle riding me
roughshod into the ditch, my brother
flying off the handlebars like an awkward angel
to land on his elbows in someone's corn.

We were so good at fixing bikes
we could do it in the dark.

On the second try, when we reached the bottom,
on the wooden bridge across the Little Kickapoo,
we were hitting fifty, maybe more.

Lord, it was grand to be young—
brothers on a bike—and though
we did it only once, at least
there was that time that we,
together, got it right.

The Sousaphonist

—For Evelyn Farbman

Mr. Vandewalker sees me coming.
I see what I want: a trombone;
I say, give me that brash thing.
I like its in-out, in-out.

But no, he sees a growing boy,
one who can hoist this python
above his head, wear it like a coat
and blow, through miles and miles
of brassy tubes, a grunting blast.

I learn to love this gourd,
its vines and valves, spit cocks
and tuning slides, and most of all
that brilliant bell that blooms
beyond its husky trunk.

Though heart often pines
at a heard glissando, the flute's
sweet glisten and trumpet's blare,
I find my compensation in order,
for I am the beat keeper.

I keep things in line. Unless I'm there,
a parade breaks ranks and turns
to a saunter down the street;
marchers meander beyond the curb
and bumble among the trees.

In the garden of instruments,
the sousaphone's a rutabaga—
bulbous, ridiculous, an acquired taste—
and few can claim to love it.
But without it, there is no Thanksgiving.

Childhood Drowning

There was the summer I nearly drowned
in Mattapoisett,
the casual victim of a casual wave,
the summer I almost drowned in Oklahoma,
and David Kloos—who watched,
in stolid amazement—the thrashing boy
and the inner tube
floating away, beyond my slippery grasp.

And then the summer in Pennsylvania
I truly drowned, in love.
I was painting my best friend's father's house
and she was my best friend's sister.

Waking from dreams of a midsummer's night,
I would early-morning rise, ascend
to her bedroom window where I'd begin to scrape,
chipping out old putty, putting in new,
thinking at the time how, on the far side
of glass and shade, her body
might curl and stretch beneath the summer sheets,
thinking how I should have something to bring—
a highly polished apple, a sweet
from the bakery at Eighth and Liberty—

how I needed a tune to sing from Lowe,
a piece of *Brigadoon* or *Camelot* for her,
how I should pry open the barrier between us
and leap like a movie star upon the carpet
of her love and take her in my arms—
strong and bespeckled in Dutch Boy Jamestown Blue.

And everything I ever did was seal
the window against the coming winter's wind,
leave a bead of hardening paint
joining sash to sill and sill to sash,
the way her father said he wanted it.

Labor Day

Continental Rubber was already at work,
blasting sulfur-stink and ashes into Erie's skies
when the morning shift came in,
slowly at first, emerging from grey porches
to walk the tracks along 18th Street toward Liberty.

Most of them just tolerated me,
a temporary botheration, the smart-ass college kid
who didn't know what anything meant:
downtime, swing shift, graveyard, killing a job.
Except Portside—a Ukrainian so named
by his foreman
because his head always tilted to the left.
Portside told me who to avoid, who'd gone mean
after losing an arm in the gleaming rollers,
whose lungs were shot from working too long
near the Vandie mills.

Today, I name these men and women
who made things with their hands—
stoppers, gaskets, escalator hand-grips—
who over years became a part of their machines:

Paolo, who fed the wringer rollers to the polisher,
catching them at the other end, moaning
from time to time above the dust and din, abstractedly,
his desperate, lonely, wordless cry;

Martha, who could peel away with her
long curved blade
a queen-sized sheet of black rubber skin
and laughing, toss it, still steaming,
back in the rollers' teeth;

and Portside, who that summer day
the United Cork, Tile, Rubber & Linoleum Workers
of America went on strike,
got his left-lolling head split by a nightstick—
the grief he earned for smearing bear grease
on the nostrils of the state cop's horse wheeling
above the crowd.

"Oh, Buffalo Gal, Won't You Come Out Tonight?"

—Erie County, Pennsylvania

At eighteen, we could drink in New York bars
and one night, in Ripley, we saw Treasure Chest West
take off her clothes, straddle Bobby Loper's chair
and lower herself on his face.

He called her his Buffalo Gal. We talked
into the night, our voices wet and dark,
and peeled the labels off our Buds.
Out of high school two months, no work,

August, 1962, and Bobby'd already been gone
a year and home from the Navy twice.
Afterward, we took Route 5 back home.
I remember, that night, Howie lowered the top

of his old man's car; it pulled us fast and smooth
by dark farms and their sleeping daughters,
past signs for Concord Grapes and Goat Milk Fudge.
WJET was playing Ben E. King,

And I recall how the moon above Presque Isle
made a golden path across the lake.
When Bobby raced past in his brother's truck,
he was hitting ninety, maybe more.

Outside Northeast, we got out in a field
and were men, by God, together and pissing.
Then, almost in Fairview, we caught up
with Bobby where his truck had missed the bridge
over Walnut Creek and wrapped itself around a tree.
His radio blared against the night
as if he had left it on, left it up to
one of us to reach around his back
to turn it off.

The Man Who Could Freeze Time

It started in college, in Ohio,
when winter dusk clicked on lights
suspended near pathways where he walked.
One night, watching girls in the library windows—
chin-propped, wrapped in their carrels,
their unapproachable sweaters—he found
he could freeze time by only wishing to:
nothing catastrophic, merely a stasis,
a quiet enormousness in which to walk.
The whole world playing statue at once—
a crashing jet stands on its nose
in the careless Pyrenees,
the mouth of a tickled child makes an empty O,
a woman leans over her belly's ledge to paint her toes
an awful red, but even the atoms
which would have danced the polish's scent
to her husband's cavernous nose have stopped.

He could do anything he wanted then—
and often did: strolling through the women's dorm,
astonished at postures the body can take,
he admired the grace of their dreamless sleep.
In the showers, adoring the unfallen water
playing halo to hair and face and breasts,
did he touch? A worshipper of rounded forms,
it was hard not to, but only as
a connoisseur of furniture would stroke

a favorite desk, remarking its shape
and handiwork, the beautiful grain.

And the pranks he could play!
Making the chapel's bulletin obscene,
shaving the Dean's mustache.
He was Ariel, Eulenspiegel, until
sated by Rubenesque abundance,
bored as a Hatter with matters non sequitur,
he'd wish things back the way they are:
the plane crumples into snow,
the child giggles with helpless glee,
the husband grumbles his way to the den.

You know the moral: how he wearied of being alone;
how the flesh of women, though warm and lovely still,
responded to his touch like wrought aluminum
and lost appeal for him, even repelled him;
how he, like Midas once, was stunned to learn
that only the dead can live without surprise.

The Doctorate

On my right is "Factors Affecting the Development
of Sleep and Wake States in the Rabbit."

> In her hypnagogic gown, she prods the hares
>   awake,
> pouring coffee down their fine blue ears,
> then lulls them off to sleep again with Brahms.

This hood across my sweaty arm proclaims a false finish,
but it is lovely, dark, and blue. This rented gown butts
against the flesh of my neck,
its blackness full and satisfied.
Behind me is "The Effect of Extraneous Information
on the Problem Solving of Non-English-Speaking
Mentally Handicapped."

> An extraordinary expert on the extraneous
> hurls bits of irrelevance upon the hosts of Babel;
> they ignore him, happily upholding his hypothesis.

The little orchestra up front makes a joyful noise
unto the Board. The music says we are processed.
A young flutist crosses her legs; her flaunted thigh
suggests a thought which makes this robe absurd.

I lose myself in the heady program notes again,
and here I find a poet in our midst: "Circadian Rhythms
of Self-Selected Lighting in Golden Hamsters."

> The little golden pigs have danced to Circe's song;
> by their own lights, they're happy now:
> their choice of golden swill upon their snouts.

My bowels quicken as my name comes near.
Is this high stage beneath me not the final one?
Beyond the lights I hear, out there, a small spanking
    of hands.
It says that I am finished: again and again and again.

Eccentric in Ohio

I would be eccentric in Ohio,
teach college English in its smallest town.
I'd wear a proper vest but let my shoes go scuffed.
A lace untied, a fly half-up, my specs askew,
I'd light my pipes with wooden lucifers.
I would make even Dryden lovable,
explain away James Joyce through algebra;
I'd bed Joyce Carol Oates with Chaucer's clerk
and outdo Donne with clever apothegms.
Amongst my peers I'd be a puzzlement,
a scourge of their committee work,
and death to their curricula.
I'd pinch their wives at alumni teas.
They'd learn to trust me as they trust thin ice:
"Look out for him—for he is very deep;
his silence opens widely like a trap."
I'd live in oak-encumbered rooms
hid deep among the elm-enamored streets
where lovely girls would follow me at night
and—oh, to be eccentric in Ohio!—
I'd close my bookish walls to shut them out.

After the Ice Storm

After the ice storm, when the sun comes out,
we hike to where the trees, like timid deer,
approach the Interstate. My younger son
dreidels across the ice, annoying his brother
and me, who break the crust and labor
through the soft snow beneath.

Emerging from the crystal heads of trees
(bedeviled and bent by winter's gravity),
we watch the trucks hitch up their heavy rubber
skirts and slalom the road with confidence.

We play Statues for anyone who'd watch:
across the ice I throw my sons sprawling,
and they freeze in antic disposition.
Trucks roar. Trees click approval with icy thumbs;
they bow to the statues of the boys.

A Father Dreams of Lost Children

I

I stand on a road which loops through woods,
in a line a hundred men long.
At a word, we enter the vaulted green,
like sad druids holding hands,
forcing the sumacs with shins and knees.

A helicopter thwacks and roars
across the tree tops like an angry angel,
tossing and tearing the crowns of oaks;
men lean from its belly with insect eyes.
Guardsmen march the perfect yards,
probe the sandbox, the garbage bin.
At dusk, orange-slickered men loose their
great, slavering dogs to bell away the night.

Fear is the dent a small form makes
in the ground beneath a birch,
hid by slightest courtesies of scraped earth,
skittering leaves and ferns.

II

I'm upstairs, my sons down playing
where something scratching at the door
does what horror does along the neck.
I dream the door chain rattles me awake,

that I run to the stairway, naked,
that I make a sound, not loud enough,
never loud enough. . . .

   III

I wake and feel for the world
like a weary swimmer hoping land will rise
beneath his feet. I sit on the bed's edge,
then shuffle off to count my sons,
to seek the comfort of yellow squares
the street light prints on the front room rug.
Here I pray for the lost child,
for the child I wish were only lost.

For My Son John

I

I think of Yeats,
looming over his sleeping daughter's head,
praying that she grow semi-beautiful, semi-bright—
not to distress her father's manly mind and
    others' hearts—
and I wonder what to wish for you;
how much of this man's wit, this one's charm,
another's courage, another's looks—
those things you'll need to catch the girl and
    keep the job
and have or not whatever a father
can pray this night, over this bed.
But before I lose you to this freak
of pasted parts of others' lives, I want to ask
how I can hold and keep this hour
as the moment and you grow away . . . .

II

Your mother's grandma sits amazed
among her scattered photo books,
trying to fit a frenzy of names to a crowd
of suddenly strangers' faces.
Her great veined hands sweep through the air
and, like light birds, pick at blossoms
on her flower-printed dress. Her mind flies up
as she retells how, fifty years ago,

she paid two hairy Irishmen ten cents apiece
to lug her china chest
up four flights of stairs to what
she tells me was her heaven in the Bronx.
But her son's dear name and her husband's face
are gone—grown out of her mind like lost hair.
"We weigh our love in the space it leaves
when it's no longer there," she says,
and the birds begin their lovely flight again.
She stacks the albums on the piano's back,
asks if I'm Italian, which I'm not,
and, disappointed, goes to stir some sauce
in an empty pot on the cold stove . . . .

III

Some years from now when you forget to write,
shall I live in a box by a ringless phone?
I'd rather learn to catch this hour and
hold it in my head forever:
I could catch it again in a child's smile,
the soft-grass dancing of a foal;
I would hold it forever in a rose's bud,
the way a breeze will play with hair,
the laughter of sun on the sea.
A father knows by loving how to lose.

On the Death of My Son's Golden Hamster

Reginald's trip-hammer heart is still,
his soft fur cold. Golden, as hamsters go,
he lies curled, fetal in my son's palm
toward dreamless sleep.

Now, night train-bound for the kingdom
of worm and mole, the little pharaoh
has gone nocturnal with a vengeance,
his circadian dance all done.

In the yard, I scrape away the leaves—
yellow birch and scratchy oak—
and hack away the spent chrysanthemums.

It is night and late, but there are things
a father ought to say at times like this—

Who knows what saves us from saying them?
Or why the father is the one who turns away,
who'd like to wish away this little death?

Transparency

My son has accidentally loosed his parakeet,
mistaking air for window, as we sometimes do,
smooshing our nose against the sliding door.
But the bird is gone: how she taunted our cries
of "Bluebell," eluded the aspen's grasp,
then deigned to melt her color in the sky.

Good fathers know the words to set things right,
but Connecticut's winter nights ahead
hold no mercy for a tropic bird.
Reality's an owl, not words, I think,
wondering if my son has learned to trust
transparency less than he did an hour ago.

At his age, once, I joined my Boy Scout troop
searching the lagoons for a man
who'd slipped beneath the early April ice.
Tied to friends on shore, I bellied my way
toward a ragged hole until a sheen
of glass was all that supported me
above the weeds, above the fish who watched
me scuttle like a water walker
through their sky. Pressed against the pane
of what seemed clear enough to both of us,
I found my mirror man, his pearly eyes
wide open to the slowly melting world.

Shenandoah

— For Jeffrey and Micki
5 August 2000

In the movie, James Stewart appeared in a heavy coat
with enough white fleece across his chest and neck
to clothe a flock of sheep. In that coat, on horseback,
he blocked out half the blue Virginia sky. In the movie,
there were wedding plans, but awful things, too, an
unspeakable war between brothers—I can't remember.

What I do recall is how, in James Stewart's speech,
there was always that gap between longing for words
and the instant they'd come to the tip of his tongue,
as if each word were a gift. And that coat.
I bought a coat like that and wore it for years.
I even thought I'd worn and thrown it out
until one day my second son showed up in Utica
wearing my Shenandoah coat. It pleased me—
to think of him wading through deep Mohican snows,
the ragged fleece pulled up against his neck, wrapped
like a clapper in the bell of a buttonless coat.

And then there was the word itself.
Imagine the first Shawnee who needed a magic word
for the wedding of tree and sky, for the way a river
washes against the banks of its valley, making anew
a new home for itself, a full-voweled word for how

a deer nudges its fawn to drink at river's edge.
Shenandoah. She mouths it, and it means all the
moments in a river's life, its seasonal coming and going,
its picking up and putting down.

Now, James Stewart, I need a single word.
I need a word for that sharp intake of breath
when a father sees someone become a man
stepping through snow, so much like himself
in a familiar coat. I need a word for pride, for love,
a word for the moments when life lets go of itself,
like that second we released our grip
and our child rode beyond the edge of surety,
like that time we wept all night, having left him
   at college;
and now for this moment beyond waiting:
when he puts down the coat of his parents' love
and wraps himself—from all the world can offer him—
in another one, this one to last a lifetime.

The predictable words may be too hard to say,
too long in coming:
Shenandoah, Jeffrey, Micki. Shenandoah.

Devices

—For John and Mary on the occasion
of their wedding, 27 June 1998

These devices we've gathered across the years—
our lives cluttered with charms and inoculations,
amulets, unguents, salves, balms,
palliatives—drawers crammed with first-aid kits,
pads, helmets, goggles and guards—
all the policies sold to protect us
against eventualities in your life,
to your limbs—are nothing compared
to the plain hard work of lying in bed
whenever you were out at night,
concentrating on keeping your car
on course and clear of ice and drunks,
your seatbelt tight and you awake.
No plastic saint could prove
more faithful or effective.

We childproofed our house, your life;
there is no sharpened edge
we didn't find and mollify,
no germ or parasite
for which we would not sell our souls
to find the necessary antigen.

When you went off to college and we,
not knowing what you did or where you were,
were left imagining, I remembered
the film where John Travolta,
unarmed against a world of woe,
grew up in a plastic room.
I was the father, dismayed when the boy
at last got out: my heart began an errant
beat kept by a fourth-grade band.

It's not exactly that we're tired,
but when we see photos
of you wind-surfing and you tell us
about skiing in Switzerland, sculling
the Skuylkill alone at dawn in a brewing
storm, and biking the streets of Philadelphia,
we know the safety's off; we are no match.
We have enlisted help.

Mary, disarming new daughter,
we've finally learned that worry and love
are not the same. We would, if we could,
consign to you the first and keep the second.

This sounds a lot like prayer:
Mary, help protect what's dear to us
until we're gone: that brilliant head,
those strong, straight limbs.

But I suspect it doesn't work that way.
Go live, the two of you,
go run your heedless ways
and never mind the two of us,
the hours we spend awake at night,
our closets groaning, overstuffed with
these useless protective devices.

It's all we ask of you, for you:
Stay happy as you are this day,
stay deep in love—
and if you love us too,
stay safe.

Arturo and Stella

Nothing the uncles said
about how Grandpa, single-handed,
shut down the mills
or the time the quarry owners
tried to blow him up—
nothing they said
the day he died
meant as much to me
as remembering the time
I went upstairs and saw
him stooped to labor
with scissors and files
on Grandma's yellow toenails—
like Carrera marble, he said—
and Grandma crying and laughing
both at once
because it hurt and tickled so.

Americana

I

Years from now, scientists will gather in my
    basement
to ponder the sinking of North America and discover
these old encyclopedias. Like family Bibles,
these books can't be discarded, and like soldiers,
they shoulder towards a black hole created
by the general collapse of the world's wisdom.
There is no mention among them
of the stranger, the single, shimmering disc
that makes their bristling canons obsolete.

II

My father told me there once was a man
(sometime before Shakespeare this must've been)
who read, before he died, all there was to read.
Imagine being a student without a major,
being the last to know it all, sensing how
the business of knowledge would fall among
squabbling departments, that you were the last
to write, whenever you found time to write,
across the whole curriculum.

III

Mustering toward mold and ruin,
these books uphold their clear divisions.
They keep Descartes in his place,
stop him from meddling with Kant and Spinoza.
It speaks volumes, how a family secret
is betrayed in the swelling of A and C and M,
the relative slimness of P and Q and R.
The letters toward the end are diminished cousins,
huddling between their covers for warmth.

IV

My father-in-law bought them.
I picture him, Silvio Libero Massolo,
beaming with youth and family pleasure,
unpacking his new Americanas,
removing the sheer tissue, loosening the bindings,
slowly and carefully spreading them open,
according to instructions, arranging them afterwards
on the shelf. How he must have loved them,
the brilliant burden of all that knowing.

For Maria Oneto

—On the Occasion of Her One-Hundredth Birthday

I

Picture an evening ninety years ago:
Genova in springtime; small boats,
returning home, lightly knock against
the evening calm of Il Mare Liguria;
Piazetta San Matteo, empty now,
delicate pink palaces blessing Via Balbi,
background mountains catching the late sun—
they exact a hush, a reverence,
so even the sea gently slaps the noisy stones.
A girl, Maria, lighter than the call of birds,
races lace-lined waves until
a scudding cloud menagerie shadows
the inlet which contains this scene.
And though the sun will lower soon
to set on fire the leaves of olive trees
which straddle the closing ridge, it is already night.

II

Picture now an evening, only weeks ago:
a room in New Haven with big chairs
and a tiny, century-old woman. My sons wrestle
on the floor near her swollen feet
and will not be instructed to take care.

When she speaks, I do not understand,
and when I talk, she cannot hear,
so our conversation goes on—she sings, I roar.
Clumsy aunts come to rescue her from me,
to help her move from room to room,
hoping for chairs in their rightful place,
for scatter rugs to obey their feet.
I do not help because I fear such fragility.
A stupid suitor afraid to touch the one he loves,
I am in awe of her, of what she knows.

III

So what is left for us to give but praise?
I write for her who cannot read,
say lines for her who cannot hear.
It is otherwise only a matter now
of waiting and courage and listening . . .
for lap of waves upon Ligurian shores,
for knock of boats against their homely piers,
for cries of birds against the pressing dark.

Claustrophobia

It is a tightness, like a gathering of birds
in a small space, their feathers
madden the air until something must yield,
a window or wall, to a larger vista,
or surely the birds must die.

One time, my wife's Aunt Gladys,
claustrophobic, was trying on a gown
and the zipper stuck. Freezing the clerk with a
    shriek,
she grabbed a shears and did her own Caesarian,
delivering herself from fear.

One knows to avoid theater seats too far
from the cheerful glow of exit signs,
elevators, tunnels. But the fear sneaks in,
blurs like a hawk's shadow
over the dovecote, catches the heart.

Another time, I saw Aunt Gladys
balk at driving through a woods
wide as Connecticut. The trees
bent over the road in leafy conversation,
making an arch too close, she said.

What escape if all outdoors can be too tight,
when the heart pounds on a ribbed wall
until it's underground, nailed down?
We must learn, with grace, our exit lines and take
some comfort in a piece of cellophane which,
nudged by a sleeve from the kitchen sill,
scuttles across the lawn, lifts on a breeze
to flirt with elms which grace the park,
then disappears around a wall,
soaring, you know, to glory.

The Walkers

In my father's home movies
people weren't allowed to stand
and fidget foolishly.
"Act natural," he'd say,
directing us to pass the camera.
And so we walked—
the neighbors, friends, and kids—
as if there were a scene
somewhere behind the watcher,
some country we had to be getting to.

When we lived on Carol Street,
the old Italian papas,
proud in their Sunday coats,
steered their women in a parade
of good intentions
up the sidewalk toward
the Brooklyn Botanical Gardens.
Thanks to my father's movie,
they still walk toward the light—
locked in their singular focus,
frame after tiny frame—
until they disappear
and nothing is left
but the blooming trees
waving their willowy hands
against a wrinkled sheet of sky.

My Father, Who Spoke in the Tongues of Exile

After the Revolution of '56,
the Beczes and Decsys moved next door—
Sandor and Janos and their quiet, dark-eyed wives—
guests of our church. I remember you
standing before the porch at their new home
to ask if they needed anything; you began
to borrow their middle-European crunch
of consonants; you began to sound Hungarian.

Years later, as we talked with my brother-in-law
from Tennessee, I heard that sweet drawl
enter your speech like Smoky Mountain haze.

You could make most any tongue your own:
the cockney of the church's janitor,
the vocalic lilt of a student from Japan,
the harshness of Uncle Heinrich.
Once, at the bedside of old Miss Reed (struck dumb
by stroke), you spoke in silences for her.

But now, Father, speak to us at last in the language
of your birth town, Burr Oak, Iowa (sprinkled,
if you will, with accent marks from Danish farmers
who loved you, whose sons at war you prayed for).
Say the benediction in your own sweet tongue,
that deep-voiced, pastoral, American pitch.

Somewhere in Iowa, 1903

My sister Mary sends a photograph
she discovered in a box beneath her bed:
in sepia obscurity, my grandfather
relaxes in his living room. It is Iowa, 1903,
and heavily laden with darkly papered walls,
curtains, a furniture we think of now as squat.
An enormous fern glowers in the corner.
Charles Wallis, unsmiling in his winged chair,
is holding the paper he published every week
for twenty years until he died of Spanish flu.
But he seems to be studying a painting
on the wall as if surprised by its presence there.
Drawn by my grandmother a hundred years ago,
it depicts in soft pastels a willow gracing the bend of
a river, shading a rowboat, red and worn, that's
juxtaposed against the green of far-off fields
where cows can linger on this summer afternoon.

My father could tell us—and often did—
what inspired this scene, the name of the quiet river,
the town it was near in Iowa. But the facts of
the place are buried now, with him and with my
other sister, who paid attention to such things my
father said as dates and names we could attach to
long-lost fields. Now the painting's in my living
room, and I am vexed, admitting the name of the
place is gone.

I imagine my grandmother standing above this scene, wherever it is, choosing her colors wisely, trying to get it right: red barn in green field, same red as the boat, the translucent willow, the way light belongs to the river, as it always will, wanting to capture these specific shapes, both placing and pleasing herself and her young and handsome husband, Charles, wherever they lived—in 1903 in Iowa.

Mourning Doves

I don't know where they live at night—
they're too heavy, their feet too big and pink
to cling to branches—but often I lie in bed at dawn
attuned to their lamentations, and together
we brood on the news of the world.
A crow will yell at them to shut up, to give
the rest of God's work a chance to sleep.
Later, on my way to work, I see them bobbing along
beside the road, wary of neighborhood cats,
sociable as ladies after choir rehearsal.

My father could mimic their murmurings.
He'd blow into his large cupped hands
and out would come a note so sadly Presbyterian
and true to them, the birds would turn their heads
and soon the air was busy with their litany.
What false communion could he give them?
What solace did he offer for the loss of eggs?
Every morning, I see them back at roadside,
these pitiful fists of grief,
picking through the same small stones.

At the Garden's End

One summer, the pumpkin plant sent a feeler
up the cherry tree and blossomed
into fruit some eight feet off the ground.

By August, the tree complained about its
uninvited guest until my father propped
the moaning branch with a pine board.

A man from the paper took a picture
of my sister pointing pumpkinward as if she were
commanding that minor moon to stay aloft.

That autumn, grackles stole no cherries
from my father's tree; they feared
that gong of squash, that simple golden lamp.

The Fiftieth Anniversary

After heavy rains, after the grandsons leave,
evening broods softly on the cabin's roof,
filters the conversation between a sister and a cousin
who've taken to sleeping on the porch, the sound of
    dripping
from leaves, a page turning in lamplight. Above us,
my parents begin to talk. Their language spills over
the rail of the mezzanine like water, soft yet strong,
the voices of people who no longer hear as they used to,
like the bodies of small children who run naked
into a room of formal company, unafraid.

For half a century, the same voices: in Illinois,
among the scents of hollyhocks and iris;
up from the cool basement in Oklahoma;
down the long hallway of Pennsylvania on Eighth Street,
the divided stairway on Seventh;
the central double-chimney of Girard,
to settle where spring begins, in Tennessee.

Naming their homes is like suddenly recalling names
for things you can't remember but know that you love,
the way the scent of something freshly opened takes you
    back,

recalls you to the backdoor garden after rain,
the corner rose bed,
peonies wide as my father's hand,
violets in a front window.

In all these houses, among the evening home-scents,
under the shadow of a towered church,
the words have woven back and forth,
about who died and who got well,
the need to buy (something)
with money that was never enough but always enough,
one of us going off to college, all of us moving away.

For fifty years from my parents' bed above,
the complaints of my father's back, my mother's knees,
have risen the stories between them—
until there's a feeling you could take away these walls
of Thunder Ridge and the roof would not cave in,
such talk is as solid as faith and will remain,
like a blessing to live in,
for as long as we shall remember.

An Old Note for the New Millennium

—*9 January 2001*

Somehow, from the sticky gears
of my parents' ancient Macintosh, a summery note
from last July disentangles itself

like a volunteer from Tennessee and floats
through space, takes root in my machine.
My sister has recently brought them a case

of juicy peaches from South Carolina
(my mother apportions most of them for jam,
some for immediate consumption).

My father is picking tomatoes in his garden
("Some of them I can for winter use," she adds)
and he tends to forget where he leaves his cane.

Yesterday, my mother wrote (six months ago),
they went to Bill and Sonny's farm: she pictures
a clutter of lawn chairs; two funny old ladies

flying a kite; the ritual, wooden clicking
of croquet; the coolness of the Cumberland plateau
and a sleepy walk through well-marked woods.

Why, I wonder, do I imagine my parents
all dressed in white, barely touching the ground?
Here it is January and Connecticut,

and I am in despair of capturing in photographs
the way frost curls on a darkening window,
how the leaden sky projects translucently

the bony shadow of our cherry tree against
the bedroom wall. And now this letter.
Before she closes, my mother mentions,

as though she can't help herself, my brother's wedding
of the month before and my parents' recent celebration
of fifty years as one.

Thanking (someone) for the books they read,
she signs herself "a tough old Lady,"
with a capital "L," ending, finally, with love.

I'm counting on it, the way time doesn't matter,
the way my parents' letters keep coming,
accidentally, from nowhere.

The Mail

My father writes to say my letter took two weeks
to get from Massachusetts to Vermont.
It spent an overnight, he says, in Maine
and must have earned its passage north to Montreal
and back, judging from stamps
and scribbles of dead-letter clerks
(dressed—one imagines—in Rockwellian gear,
rubicund, roundly appointed,
their vision blessed by a green shade).

One wonders, really, how they ever make it,
the little letters. I picture an envelope caught
on a burred edge inside the corner box
just beyond the mailman's reach
or snared on threads inside a grey bag
which sulks at the back of a frosty fuselage.

I read once of a tornado in Oklahoma
which twisted off a post office roof
to get at the good stuff inside
and delivered the mail where it wished:
Mr. Wiggins' pension check went to Mr. Waite
(who tried to cash it at the A&P),
Mrs. Sternums got a bag of *House and Garden*s
delivered through her bedroom wall,

Harry Gordon's billet-doux
became a public document,
and Pastor Winecrock's manuscript
papered the littery town.

Whatever gods protect the mail
from drooling dogs and bungling clerks,
caprice of wind, box burrs, bag threads—
I thank them now.
Praise them, I say.
Send them a card.

Uncle Charles, Not Dancing

He chooses his clothes on the basis
of their inability to dance. At weddings,
bar mitzvahs, the annual folkdance
under the windmill on the green,
he hates being perched on a folding chair
when his pants are trying to get up and dance.

On those rare nights he leaves the house,
he thinks how his favorite shirt—
with the nearly invisible paisley print—
shoulders its way out of the closet,
muscles onto the floor and waits
for the charcoal trousers to step out.

There's no looking back! It's the blending of
Fred Astaire and the invisible man,
Gene Kelly and Donald O'Connor, all one;
no surface is safe. "Socks!" something shouts,
"Bring me socks!" and socks line up—
the new, the holey, and the newly darned—
and love how the light through the blind
is light enough, and music and light
are always and nearly the same.

It's no good. My uncle leaves the spinning space
and hides in the bathroom, goes out
on the deck with the smokers and gabbers

and nearly deaf. "Move with me, now,"
whispers his shirt. His pants: "What's gravity?
What worth is decorum? Let whatever
happens happen. No god here but rhythm."

It's an honorable life, however stiff:
suppressing on familial occasions
the impulse of clothing to carry a man
to the edge of an unbalanced calculus.
When even the trees are known to dance,
success is counted sweetest
while standing among nondancing friends;
they also serve who only sit and wait.

Living Alone

My two older sisters, living alone,
tell me they're used to it—
being alone, not being my sisters—
say they couldn't abide,
this time in their lives, another body
moving the furniture, cleaning up after,
losing the remote, wrecking the schedule.
Though I notice they keep pets for company:
one, a dog with cancer and mange;
the other, two cockatiels that lay stillborn eggs.
Sometimes it hits me what it must be like.

I'm sure it's different
for one who's been living alone for long
and one who comes to it new,
like the difference
between my two blind friends:
one who couldn't see from birth,
the other, whose last thing he saw
was the back of a bus. For me,
I try to avoid the basement
where the kids used to play, and now,
decades later, I'm still finding Ping-Pong balls
behind cans of old paint, each eggshell
like a little world that was fun
and noise and full of my kids.

I find things stored, like the box
of ugly wedding gifts, silver
we never used, things we agreed upon.
I pass my shelves of unread books,
records I'll never listen to again:
a whole lifetime of things
I have no lifetime left for.

And then I feel lonely
and let the things that used to keep me company
all those years just slip away or settle,
become something that lives in the basement,
a thing I have to pass from time to time,
but never, never pick up.

The Grand Piano

The grand piano
hovered in the corner
of the living room,
rooted as a banyan tree,
a thunder cloud
that said "I live here"
and would not move.

At night, we hid
from the grown-up world
and played
beneath its belly
by the marbled light
in the floor lamp's base.

My sister, wrapped
in black and white,
prayed to pagan gods
and made up secret vows.
If we hummed just right
and held the proper pedal down,
the piano sounding board,
dark with sorrowful answers,
would sympathize.

A Photograph of Margie

In my favorite picture of her, Margie is standing
on top of Emerald Mountain in Colorado, 1953.
My other sister, Mary, and I are giggling about something
that a friend of my father's just said, and Margie
is leaning into the wind, the arms of her jacket tied
around her waist. In her checkered shirt,
she could be posing for a Soviet poster
for moral and dental hygiene.

Nothing in this picture says the word "dead."

Waiting for E-Mail

Life goes on, yes, but as if
God has decided to start over again,
this time without titanium: always, now,
that sense that something is missing,
that the bread tastes funny, that there's
something you forgot to tell someone
but can't remember what.
Three months after my sister's death
(and her birthday comes next week)
and now I do forget, sometimes, and
want an e-mail note from her.
Not a phone call: too much to ask,
the voice—Niagara, when all
you want is a glass of chilled wine.

A chatty note that begins small,
then unfolds, expands, like spring:
starts with fixing up her mobile home—
the chip in the bathroom sink,
the furnace; the skittery sound squirrels
make running across the aluminum roof—
my sister would picture tiny,
mandatory squirrel sneakers;
cleaning the closets—requiring a trip
to the Salvation Army;
and flowers, always flowers—crocuses,
irises, azaleas, the roses out back;

the weather, the car; the car, the weather;
book orders, reading to children, their parents
overlistening, just beyond the edge;
and Arnie, the beloved, deer-like dog—
what balm she might have bought against
his round of springtime allergies.

It's all I want and doesn't seem
like much, too much to ask.

Creative Writing for Senior Citizens

—South Windsor, Winter 1981

I am your teacher and I would be brilliant,
picking words and figures from the air
like the fast-talking cowboy I once saw
who bullwhipped petals from the tooth-held rose
and laced the air with tireless lariats.
But instead I feel like the young insurance agent
who seems to care too much about your health
or like the vinyl siding man
who hasn't learned his spiel, reading from
his index cards while you sit there,
embarrassed for him and forgiving him
but wishing he'd soon go away.

But listen. This is not all my fault.
What can we agree on, after all,
if you continue to insist the piece
about the little lad with golden curls
who's crushed by a horse-drawn sorghum wagon
is better than Ransom's lines about
his neighbor's daughter, stopped and propped?
Still, I am thankful for such successes
as your lines about the windowed cat
surrounded by the household plants—pothos,
burro's tail, mother-in-law's tongue.

Leaving ten minutes before the hour is up,
I overhear, from down the hall,
someone talking over-earnestly
about upholstery. Words leap from his head
and roll the hall in rounded paragraphs,
Ciceronian, circumambient.
And in a room across the way
I see the redoubtable Dr. Chuang,
teaching origami: he holds a folded bird
to his lips, just so, and blows it into life.

For Nico: What Ought to Be a Song

I no longer remember entirely those poems
you slid beneath my door at night,
dog-eared and torn in the upper corner.
But I recall their frequent dash of grace:
the cool, hard ground beneath a
rhododendron where you used to play;
your grandfather's fishing pole tickling the sky;
the line of faces in Mad Murphy's Pub,
turning together, open as tulips, to watch a train
shoulder its way through town;
a fire escape landing, how it smelled of soup
and cat food except the weekend bouquets
of arm-flapping laundry.

Once, in your apartment, you gave Laura
and me tea. We sat on the bed
pushed into a corner, darkness licking at
our ankles from beneath the sheets.
Sipping my tea from a sunburst cup,
I urged you to write more poems, send them away;
I listed names, addresses; I gestured too much.

Looking like a hurt mother, you showed me
a box of poem parts, asking what accident could
cause their bones to knit, their skin to come together.

The last time I saw you was on Asylum Avenue.
You were bent over a flop-eared dog,
tying him to a porch post. Your long hair
hid your face from me and you were involved,
perhaps explaining the weather, the rope.
My horn bleat got lost in traffic.
I waved at the dog.

Laura says you've moved to West Virginia;
you write letters she never wants to stop,
raise vegetables, complain of a cough.
I know your hillside; I'm sure of flowers there.
Stay healthy, Nico.
Save me that tea cup; write me a poem.

Guns

My student has written an essay
defending his right to bear arms.
I dislike it but have to give him an A.

I've never thought of guns as inanimate objects.
They're alive, I tell him.

Bahner's Funeral Home, when Mikey and I stole in
to peek at the boy who'd been killed by his brother,
an honest mistake, the gun going off.

Mr. Bahner had done a good job,
and the boy's temple
scarcely looked bruised.

We broke through the door,
and ahead of me,
Mikey's brilliant head
exploded into Oklahoma sunshine.

On the Campus, Late April

At dawn, before the traffic
on Asylum Avenue drowns out the chirring
of pigeons and doves, the groundskeeper
comes into work, crossing the lawn
beneath the dark of chestnut trees,
their blossoms dripping like fat candles.
Before he goes inside for coffee,
he has to sweep away
the last magnolia petals fallen on the walk.
This is why, of all the trees,
he says he likes the Chinese maple best,
how it banks on glowing leaves,
losing nothing when it loses spring.

Below the Feeder

The mourning doves
assemble at dawn
like grey, conversant hearts
to examine the seeds
the jays above reject.

If they were men
(bound by some common inertia,
some muscular grief
which mutes their small gossip),
you'd find them
in the corner firehouse
playing dominoes.

When I open the door,
their mauve heaviness
blurs to a sleek machine
and vanishes toward thickets
of kingweed and wild forsythia
beyond the red barn.

Irises

The end of May and the iris sisters
flaunt their wares like the gaudy whores
their mother said they would grow up to be.

There is no color they're ashamed to wear,
and they refuse to keep their knees together.
Standards, portals, falls, and beards,

they've accoutered themselves
in flamboyance, in wild arpeggios
of open negligee. The door stands ajar

all night, and what's inside but lemonade
(real, with seeds), cool sheets,
and sticky things to eat?

Training the Pear Tree

My neighbor has hung bottles of water
from the boughs of his pear tree. He's imagining
an easy, flat-footed harvest in late August.
Pendant, brief suspended columns of white light,
the bottles remind me of tears, though
this arboreal training is really no worse
than bonsai trees or artful topiary.

Such are the uses of natural things.
I recall an Italian father in Brooklyn
pulling to earth the crown of a backyard fig,
burying it under dirt and bales of hay
to ward off winter. And in Oklahoma,
when I was young—to celebrate the dead
and protect their homes and well-swept yards
from nasty magic, strife, and jealousy—
the poorer blacks suspended bottles
filled with variegated medicines
from the arms of their mimosa trees.

My neighbor's bottles, though,
beneath the Moonglow pear are plastic
and chiefly a burden.

I would like to sneak beyond the fence
some night to trade the heavy water
for a lighter element. Or what if
I only removed the caps,
allowed the summer evening breeze
to blow across the bottle mouths,
setting off a hymn to soothe the yard—
a little tree-borne night music of my own,
watery chords of a clear darkness.

Mock Orange

The grass has gone
to variegated moss,
the house to mold;
what else thrives here
is the chimney crack.

Except mid-June—
and our sons' birthdays,
when the mock orange
set behind the house
bursts into bloom.

We count on it.
Its small white moons
of blossom billow
right up to the window;
the scent comes through.

Christmas Tree in August

On an August night I am surprised to find a
Christmas tree, spent and brown, hiding
behind the garage. Winter was too cold
to drag her back to sister trees to die.
So I had only lugged her out of sight
and then put Christmas out of mind.
Now here she lies, nearly needleless;
the shape is all that reminds me on this sultry night
of Christmas half a year ago, with nights gone
wholly cold, the stars so clear and far.
"Christmas is warmth in a cold time, light in
a dark place," I mutter to myself. And then
I light a match to make the fir come alive again.

She burns, in a moment, with a furious roar,
her fire a final ornament. Her fine arms
fling their light into the dark, her live voice
cracks with the high pitch, and my neighbors
look from all around to guess that I am mad,
to see what kind of man, this kind of night,
would need this kind of warmth, that kind of light.

Late Evening, Late August: As for the Rest

Filling the night with false reports of fall,
the crickets never quarreled like this before.
On Pepins' Pond, the peeper frogs converse
in foreign tones, perversely dull.
Through the window, breeze- and curtainless,
the neighbor's Plymouth lobs a square of light
which slides from closet, bureau, out the door.
I listen to the footsteps on the driveway limestone;
they thump across a porch, then disappear.

I could hear more if I were up to that;
the cogent whirr of a kitchen clock,
the long lament of an ancient Frigidaire.
Without distractions—like a coughing child,
a barking dog, a rustling of the form
that breathes beside me in the dark—
I could hear across the vaulted woods,
from far-off roads, something sad and water-like
(so constant is the cry of concrete under tires,
the whining of the trucks' remorseless gears).

And finally, if I wanted to, I'd hear
way down the street, within her closed-up cape,
old Mrs. Bell, insomniac and blind,
adjusting pillows to her sleepless head.

I make this cast of the darkest sense,
an aural spinning out and reeling in;
I let the ear sort out, from all the others,
sounds worth hearing, one by one, until
the mind must close the shell of its regard,
drowned in its own attention. As for the rest—
if oaken arms, grown wholly tired,
should shudder to the mossy ground,
or some dear, rapid thing be awfully caught
in a brutal flurry of soft wings—
I let such noises fall through darkening whorls
where sounds that change
the shape of dreams are caught—
entrapped as in a lovely, sleeping conch,
waiting for the waking ear of day.

Monarchs

First one——a monarch butterfly on Lake Erie's shore,
found perched on a stone, not dead but dying——
then others——dozens of butterflies knocked to the rocks,
battered like bits of fallen flag.
Caught by an early chill from Canada
during the last of their faint migrations,
they're fallen angels, jewels from shipwrecks.

A girl picks one up and breathes on it,
adorns her jacket with it. Soon
she has arrayed her sleeves with tens of butterflies;
they slowly move and she is ablaze
in black and orange. I imagine them
lifting her off, like Daedalus toward the sun,
but she carries them up to the woods
and, like a lapidarian, sets them on the trunks
and dying blooms of mid-September.

Soon, we know, they will be gone.
In half a year, on this shore by Notre Dame Retreat,
ice dunes will grow, fed by the crashing waves
of winter storms. I used to play on them,
clamber over the roofs of ice gnomes,
though my father said you could slip beneath
the ice and no one find you until spring.
It happened once, he said——a kid my age.

When I was a boy, I wondered:
if I died somewhere away from home,
would my soul know where to go, would it
find its proper place among the angels of its kind
or lose its way, wander like a butterfly forever?

Now I think someone might find it
on a shore like this, arrange it on her arm, carry it
up to the trees where milkweed
lets its seeds go free, choking the air
toward what brown fields, what indifferent woods.

On the Campus, Early October

Below my office window, cedar waxwings,
small brown bandits with raccoon masks,
parley and feast in the cherry tree.
As if there were something important to tell,
a waxwing flies up (twice within an hour),
bangs against the window, flaps away
rebuffed and dazed, leaving a puff
of breast-down stuck to glass.
To put an end to that, I cut from black paper
a hawk shadow and tape it to the window.
By noon, the tree picked clean,
the cedar waxwings leave; the shadow remains.

Last spring, I remember, an art student
sat below that tree, sketching the carriage house
across the way. From here, I watched
her shoulders bend to something
happening on paper—ignoring the company
of robins. Under a sudden petal-fall
of white, she put her study down
and wrapped her arms around her knees,
enfolding herself like a sleepy swan.
Here, below the hawk mark, is where
my forehead pressed the cool glass,
testing the distance between us.

Frost in the Outlying Areas

Emerging from darkness,
the farm begins to assemble itself,
and the farmer's wife can see the path
across the silvered lawn to where
her husband has entered
the long aisles of the vineyard.

She clicks the weather off
and fear curls like a tendril,
like a feather of frost on the windowpane.
Well into October the lake is supposed to
keep them warm beneath its habitual overcast.

The worst thing next to hail
is a wedge of Canadian air
come down beneath clear skies
at night to do its work,
and she knows, with dread,
that a hundred leaves
beneath the backyard peach
are perfectly folded into themselves
like gold and russet parings
from an autumn moon.

In Mid-October, on First Noticing
the Absence of Summer

On the Fourth of July
the firemen sent fifty thousand bucks
in fireworks into a sky above Winnetka
so fog-bound we saw nothing but taxes going up.
The haze glowed red, yellow, purple;
the children ooohed
and the rest of us, on every thud,
looked at each other like we'd walked
into a surprise quiz in U.S. history.

If I tried to tell you how hot August was,
how it burned the edges off
most everything in its path,
it would be like trying to explain
how lost Aunt Mina got
in the Philadelphia subway system
for nearly all of August 31st
until she surfaced for air
and terrorized the black population
of South Philly with her cane.

It was like those times driving
a familiar road
when your mind snaps back
to the business at hand

and you see you've driven through
whole towns without knowing—
when suddenly, right after Labor Day,
it got so cool some nights
it was like treading water
in a spring-fed pond
with its cold pockets
moving around underneath,
catching you now and then
where you live, off guard.

And now, already, the swamp maples
are lighting up and soon the rest
will turn to flame,
their colors marching
like a high-school band
up Paulk Hill toward Kotter's Farm.

This Is Not a Metaphor

This is simply me, employing a Toro Air Rake
to free of leaves my backyard deck, amazed
at how certain oak leaves can tumble forty, fifty feet

or more and lodge themselves so fixedly
in straits between the boards of southern,
pressure-treated yellow pine. They land

stem-first or fiercely clutch like fingernails,
thus fending off finality, staking claim to life.
Yes, most will simply lie there for the nonce,

waiting for the merest gust—
electrically motivated or otherwise—
to transport them elsewhere, thus freely flirting

flippantly in air, moving tout ensemble
like their luckier cousins, autumnal birds,
pronouncing their whims and dares

in the morning light. But some
become entrenched, hangers-on:
"We've come this far," they say,

"and won't move on, no matter what."
Others are capable of leaping upwards
above my head and, catching unseen drafts,

trickily retronavigate
so I'm forced to repeat myself
in a redundant blast. You shall not escape

the Wrath of Toro, I tell them. You shall
be pushed beyond this grey-stained plane
and forced to endure what change

and crummy demise awaits. It's not for naught
we call this time of year the fall. This is not
a silly game that poets play or metaphor.

Gathering

In early November,
I watch the enormous swoop of blackbirds
as they celebrate their ability
to move in large groups
without crashing into one another. Imagine
the entire population of Connecticut, waltzing,
and everyone can dance like Fred Astaire
and no one cries *Oops!*
and flutters flustered to the floor.

Shaken from earth's blanket,
they darken the sky, lend it momentary depth,
these pointillists, then congregate on oaks
(which persist in hoarding their leaves
like veterans clutching their bronze stars).
Where are there branches enough
for this cotillion to light on?

Do they perch there recalling
the pester of crows above boys
playing baseball, do they recall
last spring's mock orange, the bastard
on Virginia Lane who failed to fill
the feeder day after day?

Or are they pure hunch, driven to air again
by a change in the slant of light?

Birds, send me January missives
from the edge of southern swamps.
I will miss you when you are largely gone,
when the everyday sky shows us nothing
but pewter. And even as songless evenings
come later and later, by March, say,
I'll go down to the hardware store,
putter among the lawn tools,
make my pilgrimage to the back wall
lined with bags of birdseed,
make the annual promise I mean to keep.

The Husband Raking Leaves in Mid-November

He rakes the ruddy maple leaves
and curses the oaks, which have lost
in the proper season their chance
for a seemly, decorous surrender.
Let go, he says. Let go.

Inside, his wife is cleaning windows
in a blur of paper towels
to match the fury of an argument
they haven't had in thirty days.
The house's eyes are clear enough,
he thinks, and when the sun comes out
from clouds, he sees himself in glass—
a piker pushing fallen leaves
along the gutter of a one-way street.
Let go, he says. Let go.

Walking Mid-November

Porch lights come on early now, and darkness falls
between the time I leave the house and my return.
Windows turn to yellow squares for catching the
still life of neighbors: watching the first of
evening news, getting homework out of the way
at the kitchen table. It's all "Leave It to Beaver"
and "Ozzie and Harriet" here. Outside, an
enormous oak leaf skitters across my path on
twenty legs, glad at last to have reached the ground.
From across the way a dog woofs, lonely, chained,
the same dog that always barks at my passing.

Another Christmas Tree Story

A lone pine greens my winter's backyard.
All summer long it's lost in shade
and forced to drink the little sun
my oaks allow it. That—
and soil of clay that doesn't like life:
witness the battle my neighbor mounts each year
to grow enough green for one grim salad.

Last Christmas Eve, after both children
were sugar-plummed away, and I'd made a
pile of toys-to-be-tossed-to-make-
room-for-the-new-ones, and the women
were off to midnight Mass, that neighbor
and I met in the back room to make our toasts
to the season, to whatever needed toasting.

We both allowed, and brandy helped, that
Christmas made things warmer. But what a thing
to believe in, such fantasy, this story.
My neighbor said he'd sooner think my little pine—
caught shivering there on the edge of the window's
     light—
could talk than believe in all of that.

So out we stumbled in the crackling air,
brandy-breathing like dragons,
to address this sober tree, to demand of it—truth.

"This pine's no theologian, sure," my neighbor
roared and shook it by its throaty trunk.
"The two of us and it will make the trinitree.
I'll be God, you be the Son,
this tree we'll make the Holy Post."

Only the lights from another man's porch kept us from
rolling to a frosty death as back we crunched
to warmth and withering looks
from wives, sisters, and mothers-in-law.

But there was nothing in the air of farewells
and best wishes that night could have warned
that in my troubled sleep that Christmas Eve
a pine would whisper me awake and draw me
slipperless through the anxious house to where,
through the back window and my red-veined eyes,
I would behold the little tree again,
drinking its brandy of moonlight,
wearing its jewels of snow,
a vision then—of what, should I say?—
touchable sadness, untouchable hope.

West Hartford, Early January

Like wounded beasts who drag themselves to streams
for a final drink, abandoned Christmas trees
line the curbs. Conical, comical, yet sad, too,
as now—unhoused, bereft of their recent notions
of grandeur except for occasional silver strands—
they wait for men from the city
who hoist them onto the beds of trucks
like carcasses.

The workers take the trees to artificial lakes,
anchor them with bags of stone,
and sink them as habitats for fish.
Thus trees have served, like the air
of Escher's print, as home for birds and fish.
Deep and dark beneath the February ice,
snails blindly creep along the limbs
that shelter now the birthing house of golden carp,
the grinning pickerel, and all those sunfish.

A Lazy Man's Poem for January

When there's so much to do
outside—rebuilding the feeder

(which cashed it in during
last night's blow) or counting

the trees, making sure none
have bolted the yard—

how can my body lie on the couch
and watch a splotch of sun

sink from the top
of the rocker, slink

down the back to the seat?
When I take my glasses off

and give in to sleepiness,
the light slips from the chair

like an old cat and basks
in a golden circle on the floor.

TV Remotes

—Reading, Massachusetts

In the backyards children are skulking with
TV remotes, flipping channels through windows
of unsuspecting citizens. Like most Americans,

Mrs. Beldegreen believes that dreaming and
   television
are much the same. Ensconced on her suburban couch
and skirting the edges of first sleep, she's not
   alarmed

to see the news give way to sailors of
   South Pacific—
who yield, in turn, to *Geographic* in which a pair of
cheetahs mouth the haunches of an antelope.

Wide-eyed, Mr. Sherman is entranced by what they'll
show on nationwide TV at night but chooses wisely
not to wake his slumbering wife.

Mr. Maguire, however, knows what's up. Whatever
happened, he wonders, to the Vandals of yore?
Whatever befell the urge to tip a cow?

To scrawl "East Catholic Sucks!" across the
schoolhouse door? To set ablaze a bag of poop
on someone's porch, then run?

When his game in overtime melts into reruns
of *Friends,* he flips it back. Then, as channels fly
by from movie to news to opera to QVC to

infomercials on juicers and muscular appliances,
he bolts for the door to show them an episode of
Saturday Night Live.

Moving Dr. Budnik

When Dr. Budnik lost her house last fall
and had to move across the street,
she called on four of us,
whose days were stuck in idle.

"Do you believe," she asked,
"in the transmigration of souls?"
We gathered early on a Saturday
and began stacking clothes, linens,
and dishes to perilous heights.
Then carried them out to the yard
where they sat like obedient dogs.
We turned the house inside out,
toted her bureaus and shelves
to a three-room flat across the way.

At two o'clock we stopped for lunch,
lounging among the piles of stuff,
and Dr. Budnik sliced bread
made richly dark with sorghum and seeds.
She served us bowls of couscous
thick with melted cheese,
and milk cold with a bubbly head.

That is what October afternoons are for,
To put out one's belongings, like birds
that need the sun to cure a moldiness about the beak;
everything evicted for the scrutiny of passing citizens.

Clearing a space on the littered grass
among the displaced lamps and chairs,
leaning up against a rolled-up rug,
we watched as Dr. Budnik danced,
her long gray hair, from side to side,
her tambourine, those checks of gold.
She made a song about a house
with windows that wept for happiness
and doors that shouted welcome
when the owner's friends walked by.

Then collapsing among the rummage
of her furniture, she cried, "Look, my friends,
there is not a thing I own that isn't clarified,
that did not get a breath of air, a shock of light.
But back to work. The evening mustn't catch us
    moving things.
Take care, my dears, that nothing loved
 is lost in the grass, beneath the falling leaves."

Night on the St. Lawrence
—For Elizabeth

I had seen darkness before—or, rather,
not seen it. Once, at Howe's Caverns, the guide
turned off the lights and plunged us—
screaming children and bedeviled adults—
into such a metaphor for death
that only saints or poets bleak of soul
would ever think of it.

        This was different:
the whole of out-of-doors conspired to
claustral blackness; the moon and stars hid
behind an arras of unspeakable emptiness;
the normal silhouette of shore and islands
against the light (parameters of river life)
became matters of mere conjecture.

And through this inky blackness, our Elizabeth—
her small skiff skimming between water and air,
jolting our spinal cords to jelly—ignored,
among other things, our pleas for moderation,
the tiny electric flickering over the gas tank,
this incredible darkness. Till suddenly
she stopped, the boat wheeling to a halt
like Triton's horse. "A shoal," she said, simply,
as if that explained anything.

Clearly she sees what no one else can see:
the ledge beneath the surface
that would sink us to a fishy grave.
We're safe now, I think:
what Elizabeth's eyes—that are their own
best source of light—don't see
just isn't worth the seeing.

> —*On the occasion of her sixtieth,*
> *With love,*
> C.D.

Cedar Creek Charlie

Charlie painted polka dots
on walls (inside
and out), the ceiling,
floor, and furniture,
and not a thing
that Charlie owned—
from gate to privy,
Chevy to well—
wasn't measled up
with tiny daubs.

Folks did wonder
who came from as far away
as Chilhowee to see
the stippled house,
and not a black and tan
in Cedar Creek wasn't
glad he wasn't painted
like a firehouse dog.
Mule-simple,
neighbors called him,
concluding the dots were
in his head and needed
using up before
he could go from
Tennessee to spot
the walls of Paradise.

The Order of Rainbows

Coincidence is the pseudonym
God uses when he doesn't want
to sign his own name.
   —ANATOLE FRANCE

I

"Life's a waltz," he said, whirling about the room,
endangering the china, the delicate dining room chairs.
"The second step demands a third—
a matter of balance, turning not falling
into loveliness, something you have to do into art."

II

"Yes, life's the pretty three-sided glass
we held in physics class," she said.
"How it layered a simple beam of light
into the order of rainbows, showing
over and over it's made of the same stuff."

Waiting

I

I've heard that some lose love as careless plumbers
lose a wrench, readers their place, or thespians
the thread of thought, but I have always lost
by waiting far too long to put my love to words.
Indeed, the terms of love weigh down my tongue—
like hunkers of toads in sweet spring mud—
until their only tense is perfectly past.
I chase my mower through a bumpy lawn,
muttering promises, mixing phrases in a blue gas,
or on Saturday morning I melt in tears
at the A&P, frightening a sticky child,
who runs to warn his mother
of a giant weeping hard among the leeks.

II

My friend Joe Larry, of an imperfect mind,
boggled by phonics, bemused by the number three,
seemed destined to stay forever in third grade,
and so he begged for me, in fourth, to wait for him.
But I didn't. (His father, though, owned
appliance stores and a pink and black Buick
and twelve years later made Joe Larry boss of both.)

But waiting never seems to work for me,
as I should know—the kids need sneakers now,
my sister hasn't heard from me in years
(such brick-like things that press upon the brain!)—
so who am I to ask my love
to wait and watch for the burst of one true word
from me, catching her heart mid-leap, mid-stream.

III

Which brings me up to what I fear the most:
that some Sunday, when the grass out back is
    finally cut
and the sharp scent of its wound drifts through
the darkening screen, I will be nursing a frothless beer,
rehearsing my speech for the thirtieth time—
the one to make her fall so soft to love—
when that Joe Larry, born of awfullest dreams again,
will pull up front in his pink/black Buick
and coming round back, before I even say hello,
he'll sell me a Frigidaire.

Safe Harbor

These are tidy waves that roll up on the sand,
and when the wind picks up, they dance
more than ravage the harbor. All the boats
stay put: the PatSea crusty and historic,
the Jersey Princess stoic and graceful,
the Bay Lady—sails down, pure elegance—
a bit of sunlight even in a storm.

There's a reason we chose to live here
at the end of the earth, in this sandy crook
that, while laid down by glacier and transient,
offers up the sweetest protection for its lovers,
inhabitants, and losers. Manuel staggers
down the street and what do we do? Swerve
the bike in a graceful arc, brake and coax
him to the sidewalk. The tides change.
Manuel will be a constant. Or Jimmy—
a lover of art, of knowledge, of prescription
drugs, and social scenes—is welcomed
midsummer in his wool vest and galoshes.

There's the artist with the palette and easel,
unpretentious on the side of the road;
the transsexual singing Sinatra; the kayaker
offering a contrast to the deep teal waters;
the merchants, the shoppers; the cooks

and eaters; the shell and sea glass collectors;
the mystics walking through numinous dunes;
there's the lonely and the loved and those living
for love in the most unlikely of places: dark,
watery, not unkind but not fulfilling.

And what about us? What brought us here?
Three lighthouses moaning in the fog? The view?
A job? Freedom from crime? Inclusion? To find
ourselves? To lose ourselves? Were we running
from or running to? Were there mothers involved?
Was there someone to blame, someone to thank?
But most important, now that we're here, do we
feel safe? Will the harbormaster tell us when
to run for our lives, board up the windows, move,
change our lifestyles? Will we fall more in love,
grow our own food, become self-sufficient,
get in trouble, fight with park rangers, sin,
deteriorate, grow sick, forget the month?

How safe is safe? How safe is too safe?
Can mere rocks prevent the catastrophic?
Can we sit in front of the windows, bowed
in the wind, and believe we're protected,
secure, embraced, ready for anything?

Doubling Up on Picasso in the Fogg Art Museum

—*Cambridge, Massachusetts, May 2004*

Across the street in the quad,
it is the first real day of spring,
and students are throwing Frisbees,
dogs are barking, and well-heeled families
are strolling the grids and angles of
sidewalks traversing the grass.

Here, on the second floor of the Fogg,
the windows could use a bit of springtime wiping down.
Our view of the Harvard quad is somewhat obscured by
a winter's worth of whitened grime,
especially compared with the brightened interior air
of the airy atrium, which, if you were a sparrow,
would inspire flight.

In the gallery to the right,
there are two Picassos demanding
our study. Their frames are affixed,
back to back, these portraits:
one has more light than you can bear—
a girl in a pink dress and sun hat
with a blue ribbon piled atop that would
constitute a week of laundry if all unwound.
Her hair is spectacularly gold
and draped across her left shoulder
to where her fingers cannot wait

to play with it. She smiles,
but you would rather she were running,
perhaps across the quad or over a bluff,
the brightly spangled sea as background
instead of this dun wall.

The other is darker: a girl,
much older than the first
by twenty years perhaps,
is staring at you and the door
through which you recently entered
her room. Everything here is
turning down; her shoulders,
her mouth, the bough of the tree
in the minuscule sketch on the wall
behind her, the shoulders heaped
with self-deprecation, with disdain for
the man you imagine has just left her
sitting here like this, who is exiting
the door behind you.

If you were a parent,
you could not help but want to wrap
your arms across the arc of these
shoulders, to whisper into the
bun of her hair that everything

soon will be better than this,
that such a bland and blockish use of shade
cannot prevail for long.

A paragraph attached to the nearby wall
urges us to contemplate
how the studies of these two girls
reveal how rapidly, successfully
Picasso adopted the tools and schools of his trade:
how the impressionistic child gave way, within months,
to the stark and photographic edges of
the woman in yellow.

The way they are framed,
they will never see each other.
The woman in yellow
is destined to look at the
windows above the quad
and hear, perhaps, the unattainable
boyish shouts of Harvard men
and the yapping dog.
The girl, her obverse little friend,
stares forever at a cubist rendering of trees,
immersed in the colors of spring,

needing for its full appreciation
a glass of Chardonnay,
soft cheese, some bread.

So the woman in yellow
is doomed never to see
the child she might have been,
(or so we might surmise, except
for the darkness of her hair and
the grim set of her jaw);
and the child will never have the chance
to glance in the window or door
to consider how so much melancholy
came to be distilled, contained, and studied here.

The Daughters of Men

Walking the streets of Provincetown with my wife,
we don't walk exactly, rather navigate,
sometimes stepping off the curb to hazard
the bumpers of slow-moving Jeeps in preference
to the mayhem of rollerblading kids
and arm-in-arm couples of similar gender,
who step aside for no man.

But the girl just ahead of us for the last two blocks
is so sad, beyond all measure, as sad as she is beautiful.
Her eyes are dusty as the moon;
she would step through me if I got in the way.
She sometimes walks off by herself but often reaches
for her father's hand and tangles her fingers in his.
Her older brother is stupid and deserves to be
punched on the arm that way
when he gets too close to her.

I am suddenly struck by the ineffable sadness of
young girls. I see that her father has grown immune
to this condition and no longer wonders what could
make his daughter smile. She is too wrapped in
her mantle of mourning to frown,
but her countenance
belongs on a much older woman who's waiting for
a bus to Hartford, and she clearly would rather be

anywhere else and not inside her body on this street
(where, someone whispers behind us in awe,
last winter the drag queens wailed as their
thousand-dollar gowns went up in flames when the
Crown & Anchor burned to the ground).

If this were my daughter, could she ever survive
the weight of my expectations?
I would buy her whole boxes of happiness:
I would enter these storefronts and buy a mauve
sweatshirt that says "Bitchin' in Provincetown"
and a mug proclaiming "My Parents Visited
Provincetown and All They Got Me Was This
Lousy Mug" and toys (three-hundred-dollar
kaleidoscopes) and smooth colorful stones
for the pockets of new jeans with holes already torn
in the thighs, and an electric fountain for her
    bedroom
with a unicorn and a naked lady, and some shells
from Sanibel—and then there's an open doorway
with leather things, but no.

I never had daughters so I still have money
for my and my wife's hot chocolate, which we drink
on a deck overlooking Cape Cod Bay. It is the
second-best thing in the world.

The best thing is to be the father of grown sons
who make me sad but at a distance.
I remember taking my boys to the dinosaurs
in New Haven, how we held hands in that monument
to calcium, and they ignored my thoughts about the
spoor of such a beast and simply worshipped
that ship of bones. Yes, there was the gift shop
afterwards, but that was compulsory ritual
that had little to do with *happiness.*

With a daughter in tow, I'd've had to buy
       the goddam stegosaur
or, for a necklace, wrest (like a mad dentist)
a brownish tooth from the jaw of
       Tyrannosaurus Rex,
come back at night to steal the wooly mammoth
from its diorama and truck it home for her.

No, there's nothing wrong with me
that walking by the sea with my wife and
drinking hot chocolate on a cold day in April
and hearing that girl laugh wouldn't cure.

The Sloth Remembers

The sloth remembers, late in life,
a sweet attention paid to things:
the sun's high march across
the tips of the cecropia:
the scent of leaves before the rain,
the way they belly up
so moist and tender to his tongue;
and smell, too, of what
invites a sloth to love,
to meet at midden-post to mate
beneath the moon and panthered night.

But now inhere the ticks and algae
in his hair, and though he itch,
he would not scratch.
Torpid lies the air as, frond by frond
and claw by claw, he crawls
the upper story of the world,
serene in his velleity.
Old Upside-Down, Vegetable Love,
he knows what is serious:
unlike his monkey relatives,
he takes dim views of levity
and symbolizes gravitas.

Photographic Memory

I have learned to bury carefully
the images of everything I see,
or they spring up later
to litter hallway corners
like unsorted laundry:
the Venetian mural
in a motel room
south of Springfield, Illinois;
screeds of chemical formulae;
the causes for the War of 1812;
the room I lived in as a child;
the look on a woman's face
in the window of a passing bus.

I am, like no one else, preoccupied.
Beneath the black cloth
my journeyman's eye
is forced to picture everything
and bear the cost of silver,
weight of lead.

I dream, sometimes, of Charon
standing at his ferry's bow.
"Drink," he says.
"Become, like us, clear tablets
under starless skies."

But Cerberus barks at my heels
like a pet, demands remembering.
It is what I do best;
I am what I recall.

What Disappears

—Stave Island, August 1996

Some things hold on, won't go away.
Banished to some black hole, they yet survive;
thought to be lost, they hunker on floors of closets
no one thinks to open—
stamp collections, comic books, baseball cards—
there for the long duration
until they reappear—and not by accident
but as if to say they've been waiting,
wondering where you've been off to.

The opposite is *disappear:*
dunking a basketball, for instance,
like the forehand with topspin—hell,
to rise from a chair without
a cost-and-benefit analysis—
we sadly report they have truly disappeared
for keeps.

Wordsworth was wrong:
there is no compensation
in the philosophic mind.
Give me the splendor in the grass,
not silent height marks on the kitchen wall
but the mornings we made them,

not the empty-room echo of something
I should have said but didn't,
but the chance, again, to say it.

This Is Not the Poem

"This is not the poem I wanted to
write, but I hope you like it anyway . . .

——NOTE ATTACHED TO A FRIEND'S POEM

Ah, dear friend, be my sweet company.
Who knows in what deep ward
of the wrinkled kingdom lurks a perfect image
waiting to be freed, in what dark oubliette
we'll find the work full-blown, lovely,
ripe, in time——as a wild grape,
banked in leaflets, snared in tendrils,
suddenly offers itself to the hand.

A Mid-December Love Poem

We curl up on the couch, cozy as hot laundry,
watching mid-December's sun sidle down,
a sloth preferring the southern route through trees,
descending, digit by digit, the sky.

What? Asleep already on my arm?
If so, I beg the sun to stay the dark;
before the trees diminish into sky
and all horizon's gone, I'd ask to know
what watch I have to take tonight.
I'll see, here, someone's hair
glow in sun's last touch; her hand—
clenched and sure as a small rock—
makes a shadow over my heart.

Spectacles

Picture this photograph of a race's finish line,
the instant just before the tape is burst:
the straining chests of men define themselves
against the sudden brilliance of their shirts;
the muscles of their thighs and upper arms
pronounce their steely, perfect armatures;
their hair shakes out a crystal aureole,
and lips and cheeks contort against their teeth
in the needful strain that's called upon to win.

But beyond that, in the background stands
what you must guess to be a man, perhaps in a slicker,
looking downward in a dubious way
at a silver thing you take to be a watch. Behind him—
faceless, largely colorless, uncomposed—
other human forms assume vague shapes
of rest or random energy, as they will,
and further still, a slope of what must be trees
confines the scene within its careless arch.

If this instead were life, as those of you
with keener sight than mine have always known,
your eyes could choose among a stenciled shirt,
the handheld watch whose hands hold still the time,
the leapers and hurlers who populate the middle ground
with graceful, gainful strides and strokes,

or (finally, with a thoughtless shift of gaze)
the talking shapes of querulous aspen leaves
which fret the furthest curtain of your sight.

Consider, though, my boyhood years
before my face first felt these glasses' weight,
when the world lay veiled beyond my own myopia
much like the background of a photograph
as I've described above: awash in glaze,
a doorless room of frightening Monets,
a space bereft of any clarity
and yet embarrassed by transparency,
a world where nothing's ever quite resolved.

Saint Lucy, thank you for such spectacles
as this true world affords. Preserve for me
the close, the middle, and the further ground
and save my sight for more than printed words.
Protect from blurs the dove's sweet flight
as he carries my eyes from here to there.
Let there be lenses for the dance of clouds,
for the holy spray around the leaping trout,
for the far leaf, trembling with precision, alone.

The Calling

Sometimes, when I know she's not home,
I call her there, causing phones to ring
on her bedroom floor and kitchen wall.

I know what happens then:
how the cat wakes up in the shadow, her sun spot
having slipped from under her
clean as a magician's tablecloth;
how she lions her way to a southern sill;

how a child's book, balancing the morning
on a dresser's edge, decides it's heard enough
and splashes its humpty-dumpty self to the floor;
how a floorboard creaks like a hip,
adjusts itself to the house's shrug.

If I were there, still and blind
as a shadow beneath the stair,
I could hear a sympathetic piano string,
feel a faint reverberation
in the loosened French door glass.

(A neighbor woman, breeze-blown,
Greek and plump as an olive,
hoists a spinnaker sheet across a line;
she counts the rings,
figures there's no one home.)

This is a kind of love:
filling the rooms of an empty house
with the pain of no one getting hurt.

Among the Roofbeams:
A Meditation Upon Fiberglass

Avoiding the nails that want to make
my head a holy sieve, I crawl
from joist to joist, aloft on the wisdom
my wife shouts up that with a slip
of either knee my legs will serve
as hanging monuments to frugality.

Under the rooftree, where the house's fingers
touch in earnest thought, I sniff
for the trapped bouquets of bread
and coffee, for wild evaporations
from bathroom and soap. I take a count
of creak and shift, day-shout and night-breath,
wasps and their tiny chain saws.

Sad, arthritic monk,
I dawdle in prayerful attitude
above the farthest corner of the living room
and ponder upon this fragile ceiling-sky
the truth of a phrase—crawl space—
and the paradox of feeling darkly safe
which hovers above our daily lives
and suffers our light conspiracies.

I crouch and cogitate, practice my father's
old, familiar prayers that comfort me.
Ghoulishly, at last, my wife's head
pops up in a shaft of light,
bobs outlandishly on waves of fiberglass:
"Where in the hell are you?" she demands.

I'd mingled with the household ghosts
and nearly got away.

The Newly Retired

My wife claims I shuffle, that I surely shall wear out
either the hallway rug or the new leather slippers I got
for Christmas. She's betting the whistling sound my feet
make against "Warm Embrace," Home Depot's
finest nylon carpeting, outlasts the combination
of rubber and leather that soles me in for now.
I have learned where and when the sun comes in and
know, like a cat, where to sit or lie down in the
glowing puddles it makes at certain times and
   slants of day,
chasing its warmth around the house.

The sound of my feet takes me from morning light to
lunch and beyond into the broader avenues of afternoon.
I have made promises to afternoon, accomplishments
the day has learned it cannot count upon.
Myself, I count on the hallway rug that leads me
from bedroom to the business end of the house
to get me back at night.

Let the nights take care of themselves.
All I need to know of night is how to wake from it,
to put on a grateful if not jolly face as I slap another
marathoner's number on the back of the day
as it shoulders by in its lithely, crowded
host of sleek Nigerians.

They say we must get out, one of us, every single day,
or retirement will drive us mad. Staying in is easier,
I must admit, though I pine for spring when moving
the bedroom air to the front of the house one lungful
at a time should prove a little less laborious.

II

Wearing their slippers and sweat suits,
the newly retired, as the holidays approach,
walk from room to room in their homes.
They notice the way the winter sun, by noon,
already lies in a hopeless puddle under the coffee
table in the TV room. Objects that have gone
unnoticed for years while the newly retired were
working—those who taught English and fought fires,
those who wrote for newspapers and ensured
domestic tranquility — take on a nearly palpable
melancholy. The newly retired are apt to move their
furniture about, without a due regard for aesthetics or
delight, disturbed as they are by how the light is
trammeled by the terrible traffic of table legs.

Friends keep advising them to get out of the house
at least once a day, so they begin to populate the
nearby mall, sometimes walking vigorously,
sometimes snoozing, their chins resting
in the cup of a hand or against their chest,
in the few widely spaced, barely padded benches.

Differences in Light in Late May

Here, when slant of afternoon in May
burnishes the poplar at the driveway's bend
and aspens brush the window's edge,
the shadows, drenched in silver on the wall,
practice their intricate leafiness;
they celebrate and organize the light
to something I can try to understand.

I know, at her house, how the same light
angles down cloud edge, spills
through the crown of a neighbor's oak
into the kitchen window, applauding
the dance of her hands.

Suddenly, she'll lift her face toward light
and her hair will glow the way it must;
her husband, from the darkened dining room,
will see, then raise his fingers to his lips.

The Loneliness of Inanimate Objects

—Danby Four Corners, Vermont

Two hundred miles away
and aimed toward dead of winter,
I think of what I left
at my brother's summer house . . .
where now, I imagine,
my sweater is beginning to conform
to the back of a chair and the pale light,
getting its proper slant on things, leans
through a fractured hexagon of glass
(turned chalky by years of moonlight,
dust, and spiderwork)
and pushes the shadow of a walking stick
across the floor, across my brother's pitcher's mitt,
making a sundial.

Those things we left behind
measure their pottage of darkness
and light, then try on shadows
in a kind of fashion show—
first this side, then that—and thus
they make it through a winter's day
without our help but bearing up as emblems
of our loneliness—even as barn cats seem to do:
detached, alone, and nonchalant.

A Man at the Supermarket on Sunday Morning

In the parking lot I choose my cart
from the twisted baskets and broken wheels.
It must be my comfort in a sea of troubled aisles;
I lean on it, hide behind it; it is my Rosinante.
I am large—six-foot-nine, if you must ask,
and most people must—
and children like to tell me I am large,
then run to tell their mothers of a giant
lurking among cauliflowers, sniffing the cheese.

"Can you reach me, sir, that cereal, that box of rice?"
"My lady, I can reach you anything you want
if you can say what stars, what magic
brought us here together,
reaching for the same box
in this land of milk and honey and yogurt.
And where, my love, will I find pig wings?
And may I call you Cornucopia?"

I rejoice in the amplitude of women here;
I am in love with all of them.
Following their dance through God's sweet plethora,
agog with ogling, I bump their carts,
their behinds, I lust for their coupons—
except the one who rams my heels,
rakes my Achilles tendon;
I surely shall limp all the days of my life.

I steer this side of pity 'round
a small lost man with nothing to show
for his hour-long tour but bread crumbs,
cat litter, detergent, and tea.
He ponders the freezer compartment doors;
I think he's on the wrong side of them.

This is the "real world" I heard about in school,
filled with giants and feebles and heroes and fools.
"What will you do in the real world?"
Squeezing the Wonder Bread, I know
all I need to know about doing, being:
in this library of stuff which no one need return,
I've found at last more good answers
than bad questions.

Bees at the Class Reunion

—Charlemont, Massachusetts
July 1987

Under the shade of an apple tree
we lolled like cool pumpkins, watching
bee scouts test the scented heights

among the leaves. We, too, gathered
for a sweet purpose: to rehearse
and restore, to filter our lives

through scrabbled children's talk
and shards of sunlight blinking from the pool.
At first, the approaching swarm

looked like smoke from an errant campfire,
a layer in air of a ghostly something
looking for a local habitation.

But then the business of the bees
was clarified: *This tree,* they said, *is ours.*
And as to whose reunion had a better claim,

who could argue with a beard of bees
and all that venom on an apple bough?

First

Sometimes, after a snowstorm,
driving a country road,
I catch, in the corner of my eye,
a disembodied spangle
moving through the woods.
Perhaps the dust of snow on a high branch
has been dislodged by a clumsy crow
or merely lost its grip, not meant to be there long.

Who knows, but if there is a current in the air,
the snow will be a long time falling,
flirting with what glints of light it can
before it succumbs to ground or nothingness.
If I, after this, could be that, I shouldn't mind
going first.

Already now, sometimes you send me downstairs
for a certain something and I go, reluctantly as ever,
and forgetting why I'm there, embarrassed,
I muddle about until you call down the name
of the thing I forgot. What is it this time?
Mayonnaise or ketchup? Scissors, paper, rock?
Who will be first to be last? The clean electric
car that ran us down the first time we touched
is coming around the block again,
this time in a different color.

Saying Good-Bye to Someone

——For V. B. V.

I

I remember when we bundled ourselves
against the new year and leaned, like fat children,
into the cold, shivering toward the hospital
where Isabel had been dying since early fall.
The bright air tested the cheek skin
and made each breath particular and sharp.
You recalled how, in *The Ship of Fools,*
the heartsick doctor, wanting to die,
stalked the deck until, snow-blind,
he found what he was looking for.

II

From the far end of the white hallway
we saw men carrying furniture
from what we knew must be her room.
Others washed the walls, the floor.
Like alarmed birds, our hands rose in protest,
but a kind nurse came up in time, her mouth
telling us that Isabel was gone, at last.
She led us to the solarium
where a sky of cumulus horses
drove into the windows, their shadows
breaking against the confusion of chairs.

I held your head against my chest,
your long black hair over my hand.
Then we sat for a while,
as though perplexed by the pattern of tiles,
holding hands like sad lovers
who wait for a bus, a reason to leave.

III

Two days later, I said goodbye
to others missing her—mother, sister, husband—
walked into her yard, heart-blind,
wishing for lilacs to stumble upon,
finding a snow-feathered hedge of pine.
It felt like love—after the bus has left,
taking someone away who promised to write,
someone you know you won't hear from again.

The Sexton

Every spring,
he parks his pickup
in the center of the cemetery
and fills it up
with what's been left or lost
or blown awry. This year
he counts three roses
stuck in Lucite blocks,
one plaque
inscribed "Perpetual Care,"
two stars for U.S. veterans,
a ribbon with gold lettering:
"Mother-in-law."

"Like a harvest," he says,
holding a star
like a bronze potato,
scraping off dirt.
He picks from the ground
a varnished block of wood
with a photo decoupaged
of someone's dog, a Labrador—
no way to tell where it belonged—
and by the wall beneath a tree
a green beret.

Now that it's spring
the grass will start to grow,
and nothing, the sexton says,
must stop the mower
doing what he has to do,
nothing can get in the way.

Southern Comfort

SYDNEY, Australia (AP)—The universe will go on expanding forever and life will slowly die out in a dark, frozen waste rather than disappear in a final cataclysmic explosion, according to Dr. Bruce Patterson, head of an international research team at the Australian National University's Mount Stromlon Observatory. . . . "Eventually all the stars will move further and further apart and they will burn out as they use up all their fuel. We will end up with a universe which is cold and dark. But we need not worry, as this won't happen for a long time. We've got at least as long to go as has already gone before," Patterson said.

> I was afraid of this:
> no bang, no whine,
> just clinkers floating apart
> like old college chums—
> mostly flotsam, some jetsam,
> cosmic riff and raff. A power
> failure into nothingness
>
> "Nothing," says my son,
> "the opposite of everything.
> It's where the whole world—
> dirt, trees, us, and even air—
> turns fig pudding."

I throw some ice cubes
in the kitchen drain,
then sit in the living room
and listen as they clunk about,
adjusting themselves to loss,
preparing to leave, then do.

Patterson, keep God informed;
post bulletins in the usual places.
As for us, dear Australia,
we can't say we weren't warned,
but next time keep your hellish news
down under, where it belongs.

Three Months, She Tells Him

—*For Kathy Pallis*

And they say this will soon be over,
the shadows I wear inside become a valley
we both must walk.
Each morning, until then,
is a morning less I have;
each evening, an evening less.
It's always that way, for everyone,
but it's different when you count these things
on your fingers, you and a handful of friends,
a single season's worth of days.

It's spring, and morning breaks the windows earlier,
its heady brilliance swallowing, inch by inch,
the tail of night. I find it hard
to welcome days that wear a number
on their back like runners passing by.
Too early to say this is the last supper
or that's the last of anything, though I'll never see,
again, snow falling by porch light,
the fiery burst of maples in the neighbor's yard.
The other day I found myself drinking in
forsythia like wine from some exotic coast.
I would like to tell you I will miss those things
and the way grass stays green through fall
against the edge of woods out back—but

that's what people say who move to Florida,
which is not the truth.

But what is left for us to say?
Our quiet habits have worn each other well,
like a favorite coat; there isn't time to change
to something else. One thing:
if I must leave, I should prefer,
as they've promised me, a summer day,
my granddaughters running across the lawn
in their pale yellow dresses.
Have the neighborhood's old men take off
their dark jackets. Serve small cakes
and iced tea, real lemonade with seeds.
Let a good fat priest say something sweet
so my sisters and brothers feel better. Allow the sun
to warm the ground—but come out after dark,
after the children have all gone home,
and watch the stars wheel overhead—
wear a clean white shirt—
do as we used to do, a kind of dance.

Only Sixty

Only sixty, and I am one
of the innumerable old men
supporting the walls of the hospitals
in north-central Connecticut,
the lovely interior glass walls
that might or might not inform
the perimeter of a nicely treed atrium
or merely the separating device between a hallway
and, say, the emergency room waiting area,
where a West Indian woman is practicing
her endless ululation unto God,
pleading for help that never comes,
either from the angels she calls upon
or the nursing staff we later find busy
among the ER beds and basins.

Holding Tyler

Is like holding a yellow finch in one hand—
delicate, yes, even fragile,
a handful of golden song and sweet forsythia,
its mainspring overwound toward spring—
in the other, a rawboned, floppy-eared puppy,
a bundle of nothing but trouble,
all coil and muscle, tendon and whirling armature
hell-bent for freedom:

"Ladies and gentlemen! From the highest platform
ever built (known by us as Pop-Pop), Tyler will now
attempt, for the first time by anyone anywhere,
a backward Head-banger.

"Note the expression of pure joy, of ineffable
      freedom,
as he would plunge away from security and safety
into the abyss and the hardwood floor!"

It is like holding one's own heart outside of one's body:
raw muscle, valve, and pump.
If you drop it, you've bought it.
You want to contain the contrary energy,
put it back where it belongs,
safely inside your chest
where nothing's allowed to be hurt

until it's absolutely necessary due to age
and the gross accumulation of rust and incident.

Tyler is counting on quickness that no longer exists.
I once caught the body of a fly out of midair
after my brother-in-law flicked it from the table
where it grazed on spills. Reflexes like that
don't come with lifetime guarantees.

My boy, my loosely held corporation
of fledgling companies,
forgive me for clutching and grasping,
where merely preventive holding is called for.
I have learned, in recent months,
how easily life can spill beyond the lip—
of one's unbalanced cup, of one's speech—
so before we loosen our grasp upon
this little body, this boy,
we'll have to let the puppy learn to run,
the bird to fly.

All Hallows' Eve, 2005

My older grandson is masquerading as Earth,
the globe itself a singular and somewhat ethereal orb
designed to cajole candy from neighbors' doors.

"But Mommy is still sewing on the continents," he says,
and indeed the costume is missing
some of the common land masses of
Europe, Asia, Africa, and both Americas.

I hesitate to tell him that just above his heart
is where the western veldt of ancient Africa
once abutted North America, thus creating
the garnet mines across I-84 from us.

Time enough for that, geologically speaking.
In the meantime, his mommy pursues him
down the street, trailing—like a careless goddess—
pieces of Antarctica, Oceania, and Eastern Europe.
Some islands, including Madagascar, Cyprus, and
a substantial hunk of Australia, seem forever lost.

A small moon, Tyler, follows like a tiny guardian:
he's a pumpkin this year; perhaps next year he'll be
shooting for the moon, circling his brother's earth,
but this year he's a gourd, a glimmer of golden harvest,
of things to be thankful for.

About the Author

CHARLES DARLING enjoyed a 35-year career teaching courses in literature and writing at Capital Community College in Hartford, Connecticut, where he also served as the Webmaster at the college. He was the creator of a highly regarded and frequently visited Internet grammar and usage hotline located at <http://www.ccc.comment.edu/grammar/> (with over twenty million visitors to date!).

In September 2004 Darling was diagnosed with a malignant brain tumor, an event that occasioned his retirement but also created another role that he hoped to make last for a good long run: survivor. Unhappily, he died on February 15, 2006.

Darling earned his bachelor's degree in English from the College of Wooster in 1966, his master's at Washington University in St. Louis in 1968, and ten years later his Ph.D. from the University of Connecticut where he did his dissertation on the poetry of Richard Wilbur.

Charles and his wife Marylynn were married for thirty-six years and lived in Tolland, Connecticut. They had two sons: John, who lives with his wife Mary in Ohio, and Jeffrey, who lives in Massachusetts with his wife Micki and their three sons—Jayden, Tyler, and Gavin. (Sadly, Charles did not live to see Gavin, who was born in November 2006.) In the final years of his life, Darling found his greatest pleasure in being grandfather to Jayden and Tyler. In the photo on the back cover, you'll find him occupying what he referred to as "The Newly Found Center of Everything," sitting directly between

Jayden (left) and Tyler. It may help to know that Charles Darling was six-foot-nine and referred to himself in one of his poems as a "somewhat ungainly and goofy giant." It is this wonderful self-deprecating wit that can be found throughout this second collection of his poetry.

Charles Darling began writing poetry in the late sixties, and over a hundred of his poems have appeared in various literary journals and magazines across the country. Sometimes alone and sometimes with a group of poet friends, he read in innumerable bookstores, libraries, museums, and grange halls across Connecticut. He read on two occasions during the inaugural year of the Sunken Garden Poetry Festival in Farmington, Connecticut.

Darling's first collection of poetry, titled *The Saints of Diminished Capacity,* was published in 2005 and reissued in 2007. Anyone who reads the poems in this second collection will sense that Darling viewed every situation he encountered as grist for his poetic mill, that as an experience was unfolding, he was simultaneously searching for the words that would capture the moment so that it would stay fixed and not be lost. As the title of this second collection suggests, Darling—in writing these poems—was the very man who was continually trying to freeze time.

He drew on experiences from his earliest years to the last months of his life. In one poem, he is a young boy on a bike, tearing down a steep hill in the dark, with his younger brother on the handlebars, when "it was grand to be young . . . and though we did it only once, at least there was that time that we, together, got it right." Another poem recalls what it was like to be a lovesick teenager with a summer painting job, fantasizing about the object of his passions as he worked outside the window of the bedroom where she is sleeping. Other poems capture special moments in his life as a son, a husband, a father, a teacher, and simply as one who frequently stopped to contemplate the passing of the seasons and the special beauty of each moment.

In the last poem Darling wrote, several months before he died, he captures the moment on All Hallows' Eve when his young grandsons are wandering away while their mother tries to get them properly costumed for trick-or-treating. Jayden is to represent the globe but is still missing a number of continents. Meanwhile, his younger brother Tyler is to be turned into "a gourd, a glimmer of golden harvest, of things to be thankful for." These are the last words Charles Darling wrote as a poet: "of things to be thankful for." And in this collection of poems, readers will continually be reminded of how many things there are in one's life to be thankful for.

978-0-595-44827-2
0-595-44827-5

Printed in the United States
90118LV00001B/127-198/A